GUIDE DOGS

by Melissa McDaniel

Consultant: Wilma Melville, Founder
National Disaster Search Dog Foundation

New York, New York

Special thanks to Wilma Melville who founded the:
National Disaster Search Dog Foundation
206 N. Signal Street, Suite R
Ojai, CA 93023
(888) 4K9-HERO
www.SearchDogFoundation.org

The Search Dog Foundation is a not-for-profit organization that rescues dogs, gives them professional training, and partners them with firefighters to find people buried alive in disasters. They produce the most highly trained search dogs in the nation.

Design and production by Dawn Beard Creative and Octavo Design and Production, Inc.

Credits

Cover, Front(left), Renee Morris / Alamy, (top right), Bruce Coleman, Inc., (center right), AP / Wide World Photos, (bottom right), William H. Mullins; Back (top), Bruce Coleman, Inc., (center), AP / Wide World Photos, (bottom), William H. Mullins. Title page, Renee Morris / Alamy. Page 3, Photofusion Picture Library / Alamy; 4, AP / Wide World Photos; 4-5, René Clement / Aurora Photos; 6, Photofusion Picture Library / Alamy; 7, Paul Doyle / Alamy; 8-9, The Maryland Historical Society, Baltimore, Maryland; 9, CORBIS; 10-11, Comstock / Fotosearch; 12-13, William H. Mullins; 13(inset), AP / Wide World Photos; 14, AP / Wide World Photos; 15, William H. Mullins; 16, Courtesy of The Seeing Eye; 16-17, Viesti Associates; 18-19, Syracuse Newspapers / Chien Yi Hung / The Image Works ; 19, Jim Craigmyle / CORBIS; 20, Photofusion Picture Library / Alamy; 21, Stone / Getty Images; 22-23, Dan Lamont / CORBIS; 23, Mark Richards / Photo Edit, Inc.; 25, Guide Dogs for the Blind, Inc.; 24-25, National Park Service; 26-27, AP / Wide World Photos; 29 (top), Photospin.com; 29(bottom left), Photodisc / Fotosearch; 29 (bottom right), Photodisc / Fotosearch.

Library of Congress Cataloging-in-Publication Data

McDaniel, Melissa.
  Guide dogs / by Melissa McDaniel ; consultant, Wilma Melville.
    p. cm.—(Dog heroes)
  ISBN 1-59716-013-X (lib. bdg.) — ISBN 1-59716-036-9 (pbk.)
  1. Guide dogs—Juvenile literature. I. Melville, Wilma. II. Title. III. Series.

  HV1780.M337 2005
  362.4'183—dc22

                        2004020749

For more information, write to Bearport Publishing Company, Inc., 101 Fifth Avenue, Suite 6R, New York, New York 10003. Printed in the United States of America.

                1 2 3 4 5 6 7 8 9 10

Table of Contents

A Fearless Guide Dog

The morning was bright and sunny. Omar Eduardo Rivera and his guide dog Salty entered the World Trade Center. Omar rode the elevator to his office on the 71st floor. Salty rested quietly under Omar's desk as he began to work.

Omar and Salty (center) at a ceremony where Salty received a medal for his heroic work

About 10 million people in the United States are blind or have trouble seeing.

Suddenly, an **explosion** shook the office. Glass broke. The room burst into flames. People screamed. A plane had crashed into the building. Salty jumped up. He stood firmly by Omar's side. Salty guided Omar through the flames and smoke. They walked down 71 flights of stairs toward safety.

Everyday Leaders

Guide dogs are trained to work with blind people. They help their human friends do things they might not be able to do themselves.

A man and his seeing eye dog, riding on the train

Guide dogs go to work or school with their human **partners.** They lead them down busy streets and crowded sidewalks. Guide dogs go to restaurants and even to the movies. They ride airplanes, buses, and subways. They are ready to take their partners wherever they want to go, 24 hours a day.

The law in the United States says that guide dogs are allowed in any public place, such as a supermarket.

This woman takes her guide dog with her wherever she goes.

The First Guide Dogs

Blind people have used dogs to lead them for hundreds of years. The first guide dog school was started in Europe after World War I (1918). Many soldiers had been blinded in the war.

Many people who cannot see go to schools where they learn special skills. This picture of students at a Red Cross Institute for the Blind was taken about the time the first school for guide dogs began.

In 1927, an American magazine had a story about the school. A blind man named Morris Frank heard about the story. He went to Europe, where he met a guide dog named Buddy. The two traveled the United States to teach others about guide dogs. Soon the first guide dog training school in the United States was opened. It was called The Seeing Eye.

Buddy leads Morris Frank across a street in New York City in 1933.

A hospital for the blind in France, a country in Europe, was training guide dogs by 1780.

The Best Breeds

Any **breed** of dog can be a good friend to a human. Some, however, make better guide dogs than others. Golden retrievers, Labrador retrievers, and German shepherds are the most common dogs used for the job.

German shepherds were the first dogs to be trained as guide dogs.

These breeds make good guide dogs because they are smart and enjoy working with people. They are also the right size. They can go anywhere with their human partners. They are also easy to care for. Blind people must be able to take care of the guide dogs without help from others.

Labrador retriever

Puppy Tests

Not all retrievers and German shepherds make good guide dogs. At guide dog schools, **trainers** test puppies to see if they would be good at the job.

How does the puppy react to loud noise? A puppy that's easily scared by noises might not make a good guide dog.

What does the puppy do when he sees himself in a mirror? A good guide dog needs to be curious. He will sniff at the mirror.

GUIDE DOG PUPPY
IN TRAINING
ide Dogs for the Blind, Inc.

Prison inmates raise many dogs that become guides. William James shows off his puppy trainee, Polo, at a Dayton, Ohio prison in 1996.

Dogs need to be able to pay close attention to the person they're helping. If they like to chase cats or squirrels, they won't make good guide dogs.

Growing Up

If a puppy passes these and other tests, he will go to live with a puppy raiser. This person loves and cares for the dog so he will grow up happy and healthy. The puppy raiser will also teach him how to behave. Guide dog puppies must learn to remain calm around people at all times.

Buddy is training to be a guide dog. His puppy raiser, Sally, is telling him to sit.

Puppy raisers bring the animals to many places that regular puppies aren't allowed. Children sometimes take them to school. They can go with families to the supermarket. The puppies wear special jackets so that people know they are training to be guide dogs.

A guide dog puppy in training

About half the dogs at guide dog schools do not finish their training. Some have health problems. Others are too easily scared or bark at other dogs.

The Real Training Begins

By about 18 months, the puppies have grown up. They return to the guide dog school. Now the real training begins. The dogs learn **commands** such as "forward" and "**halt**."

Soon, the trainers take the dogs out onto the street. The dogs learn to lead people down sidewalks, up stairs, and around holes. Most importantly, they learn to cross streets. A guide dog must stop at every curb.

The dogs that don't finish their training return to their puppy raisers to live as pets.

After five months of training, each dog must pass one last test. He has to lead a blindfolded trainer around town. If he passes, he's ready to meet his human partner.

Human Partners

A blind person getting a guide dog lives at the school for about a month. Now it's the human's turn to be trained!

This dog guides his partner through the supermarket.

First, each blind person learns how to give commands. He or she practices for a few days on a trainer who pretends to be a dog.

Then the dogs and the blind people are paired up. The new partners share a room at the school. They become friends and learn about each other. The partners practice riding buses and finding the checkout counter in stores. Finally, they go home. They are ready to face the world together.

A guide dog helps a man walk down the steps.

A person should never pet a guide dog while he's working.

How High Is that Branch?

Blind people must keep training their guide dogs even after they go home. One of the hardest things for a guide dog to do is **judge** height.

A dog can easily walk under a branch hanging over the sidewalk. The dog doesn't think about the fact that his human partner is taller. The blind person won't know the branch is there until he or she walks into it. The guide dog must be taught to stop at the branch and then lead his partner safely around it. Together, they learn their way around the neighborhood.

Dogs have been trained to help people with many kinds of problems. Some dogs help people in wheelchairs. Other dogs work with people who can't hear.

Ready for Anything

Guide dogs have to be ready for anything. An **earthquake** in Seattle, Washington, damaged a building. A guide dog named Logan led his partner, Walter, out to safety. There were 20 more blind people inside. Walter and Logan went back into the building. They led everybody outside a few at a time.

Another time, a guide dog and his partner waited to cross a street. The man gave the dog the signal to go. The dog refused. He saw a car racing down the street. A good guide dog must know when to refuse a command to protect his partner.

Guide dogs usually work with their partners for at least eight to ten years.

This building was damaged during the 2001 Seattle earthquake.

New Challenges

Guide dogs help blind people face new **challenges**. Burke is leading his partner through **medical school**. Tyrone joined his partner, Toby Longface, on a hike to the bottom of the Grand Canyon. Other dogs have traveled the world with their partners.

Toby Longface and Tyrone

The Grand Canyon

Bill Irwin and his guide dog, Orient, walked all 2,167 miles of the **Appalachian Trail.** They started their journey in Georgia. About nine months later, they reached the middle of Maine. Irwin is the only blind person to walk the whole trail.

Guide dogs can travel for free on airplanes and trains when they are with their partners.

Out of the Darkness

The greatest gift a guide dog gives his human partner is **independence**. Blind people can get around more quickly and easily with a guide dog than with a cane. They don't need to depend on another person.

In the United States, only 2 out of every 100 blind people use guide dogs.

Guide dogs deserve a medal for their **loyal** and heroic service. All that these dogs ask in return for their hard work, however, is a friendly pat and lots of love.

Just the Facts

- Dogs are color blind. They can't tell the difference between a red or green traffic light. They know it's safe to cross a street, however, by looking and listening for cars.

- Guide dogs can be male or female.

- Some people have started training poodles to be guide dogs. In 2002, a standard poodle named Nathan became a guide dog in Britain, a country in Europe.

- Miniature horses are now being trained as guide animals. They are about the same size as guide dogs, but they live much longer. Some miniature horses can work for 25 years.

- A guide dog in Florida once refused to let his partner cross a street. The woman returned home and told her husband what had happened. He drove to the corner. There he saw a 10-foot-long alligator lying in the middle of the road.

golden retriever

Labrador retriever

German shepherd

Appalachian Trail (AP-uh-*lay*-chee-uhn TRAYL) a hiking path in the eastern United States that extends from Maine to Georgia

breed (BREED) type of a certain animal

challenges (CHAL-uhnj-iz) interesting or difficult problems or tasks that require extra work or effort to do

commands (kuh-MANDZ) instructions given to be obeyed; orders

earthquake (URTH-*kwayk*) a sudden shaking of a part of the earth, caused by movement of the earth's crust

explosion (ek-SPLOH-zhuhn) what happens when something explodes, or bursts apart with a loud noise and great force

halt (HAWLT) to stop

independence (in-di-PEN-duhnss) the condition of not wanting or needing much help from others

judge (JUHJ) form an opinion about something

loyal (LOI-uhl) faithful to others

medical school (MED-uh-kuhl SKOOL) the school someone goes to in order to become a doctor

partners (PART-nurz) two or more people who do something together

trainers (TRAYN-urz) people who teach a person or animal how to do something

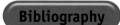
Bibliography

Bidner, Jen. *Dog Heroes: Saving Lives and Protecting America.* Guilford, CT: Lyons Press (2002).

Farran, Christopher. *Dogs on the Job!* New York, NY: Avon (2003).

Gorrell, Gena K. *Working Like a Dog: The Story of Working Dogs through History.* Toronto, Canada: Tundra Books (2003).

Owens, Carrie. *Working Dogs.* Rocklin, CA: Prima Publishing (1999).

Singer, Marilyn. *A Dog's Gotta Do What a Dog's Gotta Do.* New York, NY: Henry Holt (2000).

Read More

Alexander, Sally Hobart. *Mom's Best Friend.* New York, NY: Macmillan (1992).

Arnold, Caroline. *A Guide Dog Puppy Grows Up.* San Diego, CA: Harcourt Brace Jovanovich (1991).

Jackson, Donna M. *Hero Dogs: Courageous Canines in Action.* New York, NY: Little, Brown and Company (2003).

Learn More Online

Visit these Web sites to learn more about guide dogs:

www.guidedogs.com

www.guidedog.org

www.guidingeyes.org

www.seeingeye.org

Index

About the Author

Melissa McDaniel is a writer and editor who lives in New York City. She is the author of 20 books for young people.